How It's Done

Building a Bridge

by Kate Morrow

I0881250

FOCUS READERS

BEACON

www.focusreaders.com

Copyright © 2020 by Focus Readers®, Lake Elmo, MN 55042. All rights reserved. No part of this book may be reproduced or utilized in any form or by any means without written permission from the publisher.

Focus Readers is distributed by North Star Editions:
sales@northstareditions.com | 888-417-0195

Produced for Focus Readers by Red Line Editorial.

Content Consultant: Karen Chou, Ph.D., P.E., Assistant Chair and Clinical Professor of Civil & Environmental Engineering, Northwestern University

Photographs ©: tiburonstudios/iStockphoto, cover, 1; ewg3D/iStockphoto, 4; NicolasMcComber/iStockphoto, 7; MasaoTaira/iStockphoto, 8; Drazen_/iStockphoto, 11, 29; teekid/iStockphoto, 12; deela dee/Shutterstock Images, 14; karegg/Shutterstock Images, 16; A7880S/Shutterstock Images, 19; titipongpwl/Shutterstock Images, 20–21; SergeyVButorin/iStockphoto, 22; Randy Hergenrether/Shutterstock Images, 25; ChuckSchugPhotography/iStockphoto, 27

Library of Congress Cataloging-in-Publication Data
Names: Morrow, Kate, 1990- author.
Title: Building a bridge / Kate Morrow.
Description: Lake Elmo , MN : Focus Readers, 2020. | Series: How it's done | Includes index. | Audience: Grades 4–6
Identifiers: LCCN 2019036396 (print) | LCCN 2019036397 (ebook) | ISBN 9781644930342 (hardcover) | ISBN 9781644931134 (paperback) | ISBN 9781644932711 (pdf) | ISBN 9781644931929 (ebook)
Subjects: LCSH: Bridges--Juvenile literature.
Classification: LCC TG148 .M67 2020 (print) | LCC TG148 (ebook) | DDC 624.2--dc23
LC record available at https://lccn.loc.gov/2019036396
LC ebook record available at https://lccn.loc.gov/2019036397

Printed in the United States of America
Mankato, MN
012020

About the Author

Kate Morrow is a former teacher and writer. She has an M.A. in writing from the National University of Ireland–Galway.

Table of Contents

Chapter 1

Connecting People and Places

Construction vehicles rumble to life. Excavators dig holes in the soil. Bulldozers remove extra soil and level the land. Cranes lift steel beams into place. The workers are building a bridge.

Many people must work together to build a bridge.

Bridges are large structures. Some bridges help people move across rivers. Other bridges help cars cross highways and deep valleys. But all bridges make travel easier. They help **traffic** flow smoothly.

Bridges are usually made of metal, concrete, or wood. There are

Fun Fact

The United States has more than 600,000 bridges.

Drivers use the Brooklyn Bridge to move between Brooklyn and Manhattan in New York City.

many types of bridges. They come in different shapes.

Building a bridge takes time. It also takes careful planning. Builders need to make sure the bridge is safe for people to use.

Chapter 2

Planning the Design

Bridges carry a lot of traffic. For this reason, they must be strong and stable. Also, they must stay strong and stable over time. So, every bridge starts with a plan. Planners follow safety rules.

Cars on a bridge add a lot of weight.

These rules make sure bridges are safe for cars and people to use.

Many people work together to plan a bridge. First, city officials choose the site where the bridge will be built. Then, **engineers** create **designs** for the bridge. The designs show what the bridge could look like.

Engineers make sure the designs will work in real life. Using math, they ensure the designs are safe. The bridge must meet the safety

City officials might look at many sites before choosing where to build a bridge.

rules. It must be able to hold the weight of traffic. Engineers also decide which materials will be used in the bridge.

Engineers create a three-dimensional design of the bridge.

The engineers choose one design. Then they create drawings of what the bridge should look like. They also list any materials needed. Engineers give these instructions to the construction manager. This person is in charge of the overall building process. City officials also hire a general contractor. This person finds workers to build the bridge.

Fun Fact

Gustave Eiffel was an engineer. He designed the famous Eiffel Tower in Paris, France. But he designed bridges for years before that.

55
54
51
50

Chapter 3

Time to Build

The contractor buys materials such as metal and concrete. He or she hires crews of workers. Then bridge construction begins.

First, the workers clear the land where the bridge will go.

A pile driver is one of many machines used in bridge construction.

A concrete column attaches to a concrete foundation.

They dig into the ground. Then they lay the bridge's **foundation**. The foundation will hold the bridge steady.

The type of foundation depends on the soil underneath the bridge.

Bridges are very heavy. The ground needs to be able to support their weight. Some foundations stretch out underneath the ground. They spread the weight of the bridge over a wide area. Other foundations involve long bars called piles.

Fun Fact

Some bridges must cross deep water. Builders create a walled area in the water. They pump out the water in the walled area. Then they can make a concrete pillar for the bridge.

Piles are dug deep into the ground. These bars carry the bridge's weight down to firm soil or rock.

Workers build **supports** next. Supports are made of concrete, wood, or metal. Some supports go on either end of the bridge. These supports hold the bridge in place. Other supports send the bridge's weight to the foundation.

Different types of bridges use different supports. Some supports hold up the **deck** from underneath.

TYPES OF BRIDGES

arch bridge
a bridge that has a curved structure that supports its weight

girder bridge
a bridge that is supported by large beams under the deck

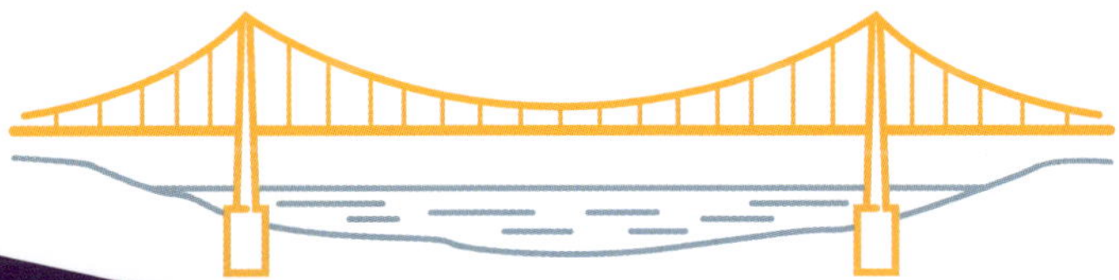

suspension bridge
a bridge that hangs from large cables held up by tall towers

For example, a bridge might have metal beams or **arches**. On other bridges, supports hold up the deck from above. Cables connected to tall towers hold the deck in place.

THAT'S AMAZING!

The Golden Gate Bridge

The Golden Gate Bridge is in San Francisco, California. It connects the city with Marin County. Work on the bridge began in 1933. Many people did not believe the bridge could be built. But engineer Joseph Strauss moved forward anyway. In 1937, the bridge opened to the public. At the time, it was the world's longest and tallest **suspension bridge**. More than two billion vehicles have crossed it since it opened. The bridge can withstand harsh conditions. It can sway sideways in heavy winds. It can stand against most earthquakes.

Tall towers hold up the Golden Gate Bridge's deck.

Chapter 4

Finishing Up

After building the supports, workers lay the bridge deck. The deck is the flat surface of the bridge. Cars and people use the deck to cross the bridge.

Workers fit a concrete beam into place.

The deck is usually made of concrete. To build the deck, workers create a grid of steel beams. They build a form or frame on top of the grid. Then they pour concrete into the form. The form holds the wet concrete in place as it dries. The wet concrete could take up to

Fun Fact

Nearly 600 experts worked on the Hangzhou Bay Bridge in China. As of 2019, it was the world's longest ocean-crossing bridge.

Workers will pour wet concrete over these steel bars to create the deck of a bridge.

one month to dry. The finished deck is what cars will drive over.

Workers add final features to the deck. Sidewalks allow people to cross the bridge on foot. Safety railings protect people from falling off.

The construction is done. But the bridge cannot be opened just yet. People must **inspect** it first. Inspectors check to make sure the bridge meets the safety rules. It must be strong enough to hold cars and people. It must also be able to last for many years. Time

Fun Fact

Bridges can be taken apart. The London Bridge in England was taken apart. It was later moved and rebuilt in Arizona.

An inspector takes a close look at a bridge before approving it for use.

and weather can damage a bridge. People will keep checking the bridge's safety over the years.

The inspectors must agree that the bridge is safe. Once they do, the city opens the bridge to the public. People and cars can now use the bridge.

FOCUS ON

Building a Bridge

Write your answers on a separate piece of paper.

1. Write a paragraph summarizing the main ideas of Chapter 2.
2. Why do you think it's important that engineers plan the bridge before it is built?
3. Who hires crews of workers to build a bridge?
   A. the general contractor
   B. the engineer
   C. the construction manager
4. What might happen if bridge builders did not follow safety rules?
   A. The bridge might not be able to hold up the weight of traffic.
   B. The bridge might be built in the wrong location.
   C. The bridge might last a very long time.

5. What does **stretch** mean in this book?

Some foundations ***stretch*** *out underneath the ground. They spread the weight of the bridge over a wide area.*

A. to become shorter
B. to become straight
C. to become longer

6. What does **withstand** mean in this book?

The bridge can ***withstand*** *harsh conditions. It can sway sideways in heavy winds. It can stand against most earthquakes.*

A. to be destroyed or toppled over
B. to survive without taking much damage
C. to be changed or greatly affected

Answer key on page 32.

Glossary

arches
Curved structures that are shaped like rainbows and can support the weight of bridges.

deck
The surface of a bridge used by people or vehicles.

designs
Plans that include the size, materials, and shape of a structure to be built.

engineers
People who design roads, bridges, buildings, or structures.

foundation
The supporting base of a structure.

inspect
To check something carefully.

supports
The parts of a bridge that help send weight to the foundation.

suspension bridge
A type of bridge in which the deck hangs from cables attached to towers.

traffic
The movement of cars or other vehicles along a road or bridge.

To Learn More

BOOKS

Bell, Samantha S. *Building Bridges*. Lake Elmo, MN: Focus Readers, 2018.

Newland, Sonya. *Extraordinary Bridges: The Science of How and Why They Were Built*. North Mankato, MN: Capstone Press, 2019.

Ringstad, Arnold. *The Building of the Golden Gate Bridge*. Mankato, MN: The Child's World, 2017.

NOTE TO EDUCATORS

Visit **www.focusreaders.com** to find lesson plans, activities, links, and other resources related to this title.

Index

Answer Key: 1. Answers will vary; **2.** Answers will vary; **3.** A; **4.** A; **5.** C; **6.** B